Original title:
Through the Veil of Passion

Copyright © 2025 Swan Charm
All rights reserved.

Author: Linda Leevike
ISBN HARDBACK: 978-1-80559-014-9
ISBN PAPERBACK: 978-1-80559-513-7

Infusion of Dark and Light

In shadows deep, a whisper calls,
Where silence dances, darkness sprawls.
Yet through the veil, a glimmer shines,
In every heart, the light entwines.

A canvas stretched, both dark and bright,
With brushstrokes bold, they find their flight.
In twilight's arms, they softly blend,
A harmony, where shades transcend.

The moon will weave its silver lace,
While stars emerge, a slow embrace.
In secret hues, the beauty lies,
In contrast born, a world defies.

As fires flicker, shadows play,
Their dance, a game of night and day.
In fusion found, they share the space,
A fleeting glimpse, a gentle grace.

From dusk till dawn, the balance sways,
In every heartbeat, love relays.
For in this tale of dark and light,
We find the truth, in our own sight.

Tapestry of Tangled Fates

Threads of time weave through our hands,
Each moment we grasp, like grains of sand.
The patterns emerge, both bright and dark,
Entwined in stories, igniting a spark.

Fate's needles dance, stitching joy and sorrow,
Weaving tomorrows from dreams we borrow.
In the fabric of life, our hearts resonate,
A tapestry rich with love and hate.

Luminous Echoes of Affection

In twilight's glow, whispers drift near,
Soft echoes of love, crystal clear.
Each word a lantern, lighting the night,
Guiding lost souls to warmth and light.

With every heartbeat, a promise made,
In the hush of dusk, we won't be swayed.
Luminous visions of all we could be,
Reflecting the bond, you and me.

Fireflies in the Dark

Dancing lights flicker, a magical sight,
Fireflies whisper secrets in the night.
They weave through shadows with gentle grace,
Drawing us closer in their embrace.

Chasing the glow, let worries depart,
Each tiny spark ignites a new start.
In the still of darkness, we find our way,
Guided by love, forever we stay.

The Undercurrents of Desire

Beneath the surface, a current flows,
Silent but strong, where longing grows.
Whispers of passion swirl in the deep,
Awakening dreams we dare not keep.

Through tangled depths, we silently glide,
Exploring the shadows where secrets hide.
In the dance of the heart, we yearn and sigh,
Carried by waves to the infinite sky.

Rhythms of Unspoken Bonds

In the silence, heartbeats weave,
A language that we both believe.
With each glance, a story told,
In quiet warmth, our love unfolds.

Moments pass like whispered dreams,
In shadows cast by moonlit beams.
A dance where words are not required,
Two souls entwined, forever inspired.

Across the miles, a tether strong,
In thoughts unspoken, we belong.
The rhythm of our souls in sync,
In every pause, we stop and think.

Through laughter shared and tearful skies,
We find the truth behind our eyes.
In sighs that linger in the air,
A bond unbroken, beyond compare.

As dusk descends and shadows grow,
In fleeting moments, love will flow.
Unseen threads connect our fates,
In every heartbeat, love resonates.

Flickering Lights of Desire

In the dark, your gaze ignites,
A spark that dances, pure delights.
With every look, the flames arise,
Flickering passion in our eyes.

Electric whispers trace the night,
A rhythm felt, a subtle flight.
A tapestry of secret dreams,
In shadows cast, desire gleams.

The world fades, it's just us two,
In every heartbeat, feelings brew.
With every touch, we break the chains,
In silent echoes, love remains.

Unfolding moments, soft and sweet,
In the twilight, our hearts meet.
A flicker here, a warmth so near,
In every breath, our truth is clear.

Through starry nights, we'll dance and play,
In flickering lights, we find our way.
As endless desire lights the skies,
In every heartbeat, love replies.

Resonance of the Soul's Embrace

In the depths of quiet grace,
Your spirit finds its rightful place.
With every hug, a universe,
A bond that time will not disperse.

We linger long in gentle sway,
In every breath, a soft ballet.
The echoes of our laughter blend,
In sacred silence, hearts transcend.

In warm embrace, the world does fade,
In your arms, my fears invade.
With whispered truths, our souls entwine,
In every heartbeat, you are mine.

Beyond the noise, we let love soar,
In resonance, we both explore.
With every moment, deeper we dive,
In soul's embrace, we come alive.

Through thunderous storms and summer's light,
Together, we shall face the night.
In the depths, our love will trace,
The resonance of the soul's embrace.

A Symphony of Unseen Desires

In the silence, music plays,
A symphony through tender ways.
With every glance, a note inspired,
In unseen depths, our hearts conspired.

Notes of longing fill the air,
A melody we both can share.
In quiet moments, we compose,
A song of love that gently flows.

With every touch, the rhythm builds,
A dance of dreams that love fulfills.
Through hidden notes, our passions rise,
In harmony, we touch the skies.

The crescendos swell, hearts collide,
In the depths, our souls abide.
A chorus sweet, we sing in tune,
Underneath the watchful moon.

As whispers fade into the night,
In music's warmth, we find our light.
A symphony of dreams on fire,
In every heartbeat, deep desire.

The Allure of Dreamscapes

In the stillness where whispers sigh,
I wander realms where shadows lie.
Stars spill secrets, twilight's gleam,
Reality fades, lost in the dream.

Colors dance in velvet skies,
Mirrored wishes and longing cries.
Pathways beckon, soft and bright,
In this world, I'm lost to light.

Clouds of silk drift overhead,
Carrying thoughts that words have fled.
Time dissolves, a gentle stream,
In the fabric of the dream.

Echoes form like tender lace,
Every moment a warm embrace.
A journey where the heart can soar,
Through portals to forevermore.

And in this place, I find my peace,
A sanctuary where troubles cease.
As midnight hushes life's parade,
I dwell in the allure of dreamscapes made.

Threads of Infinity Between Us

In quiet glances, sparks ignite,
We weave our dreams through endless night.
Tender whispers stitch the space,
Where distance fades, and hearts embrace.

The universe, a tapestry spun,
We are the patterns, two as one.
Stars align in a cosmic dance,
Fate ties us with every chance.

With every heartbeat, threads expand,
Binding souls with gentle hands.
Infinite echoes in the air,
Speak of love beyond compare.

Through the fabric of time we glide,
No force can tear these threads inside.
They shimmer softly, pure and bright,
Guiding us home, a shared delight.

In every moment, a bond grows strong,
Two hearts sing their timeless song.
Together, forever, through life's caress,
Threads of infinity, we possess.

Scent of Blushing Petals

In gardens where the blossoms bloom,
Sweet perfumes dissolve the gloom.
Petals blush in morning light,
Whispers carried, soft and bright.

Nature sings a fragrant hymn,
As daylight breaks on the world's rim.
With every breeze, secrets shared,
The scent of love, gently bared.

Crimson, gold, and shades of grace,
Each petal tells a story's trace.
Memories dance in the summer air,
Echoing moments we used to share.

Beneath the boughs, we laughed and played,
In the garden where dreams laid.
Time stood still, a breath held tight,
Under a sky draped in twilight.

Now distant blooms still hold their scent,
In every heart, whispers are sent.
When breezes touch my cheek, I feel,
The scent of blushing petals, real.

Embrace Beyond the Horizon

The sun dips low, kissing the sea,
Waves roll softly, wild and free.
In twilight's glow, we find our place,
In the embrace of time's gentle grace.

Chasing dreams that never fade,
Together, in this serenade.
With every sunset, hopes arise,
A tapestry of painted skies.

Hand in hand, we stroll the shore,
Finding treasures more and more.
Every footprint tells a tale,
Of love's journey, a sweet unveil.

As starlit night begins to fall,
We linger, lost in it all.
The horizon calls with dreams anew,
Embrace the vastness, just us two.

Beyond the edge where land meets tide,
In every heartbeat, we confide.
A promise whispered soft but clear,
In this embrace, I'll hold you near.

Whispers of Euphoria

In twilight's gentle embrace,
Dreams begin to weave and flow.
Colors dance, bright and bold,
Whispers of joy that softly glow.

Hearts flutter like butterflies,
With each breath, the world aligns.
Moments melt in sweet surprise,
As time surrenders, love entwines.

Laughter spills like liquid gold,
In every corner, warmth ignites.
A tapestry of stories told,
In a symphony of starlit nights.

The scent of blooms in midnight air,
Holds secrets held by moonlit skies.
Each heartbeat echoes, ever rare,
A song that blooms, never dies.

Together lost in sacred space,
Where whispers cradle every sigh.
Euphoria wrapped in soft embrace,
As hearts ignite and spirits fly.

The Dance of Desire

Underneath a silver moon,
Silhouettes entwine and sway.
Every glance, a sweet festoon,
In the night, passion holds sway.

With every step, the magic grows,
Fingers brush, electric flash.
A yearning symphony that flows,
The dance goes on, a secret bash.

The rhythm pulses, wild and free,
Heartbeat matching every beat.
In this trance, just you and me,
Lost in time beneath our feet.

Flames ignite with tender grace,
In the shadows, dreams collide.
Weaving threads in this vast space,
Where desires cannot hide.

And in the morning's golden light,
Memories linger, soft and bright.
Every heartbeat, a sweet refrain,
In the dance where love remains.

Secrets in the Dawn

At dawn's soft break, the whispers call,
Stories of night begin to fade.
Sunrise paints the world so small,
In its warmth, secrets cascade.

Golden rays kiss the sleeping earth,
As shadows melt into the clear.
Awakening moments hold such worth,
Each breath a promise, crystal sheer.

Birds sing softly, tales anew,
In the light, mysteries unravel.
With every glance, a spark so true,
As we embark on the joyful travel.

Memories linger, gentle and bright,
In the embrace of day's fresh start.
A tapestry woven in morning light,
As sunlight dances in each heart.

The world unfolds, and dreams take flight,
In the grace of dawn's revealing light.

Shadows of Ecstasy

Beneath the stars, whispers ignite,
In the dark, where thrill takes form.
Every glance feels pure delight,
Within the shadows, passions warm.

Echoes of laughter, faint and sweet,
Breathe life into the midnight hue.
As desires rise and hearts compete,
In the quiet, only me and you.

Crescendo of dreams whispered low,
Each touch a spark, igniting fire.
In secrets shared, pleasure will flow,
In this realm of pure desire.

There's magic woven in the air,
As darkness dances, time stands still.
Lost in the night without a care,
Yearning deep, yet hearts refill.

In shadows spun of ecstasy,
We find a world of mystery.

Whispers of Desire

In the stillness of the night,
Soft secrets softly tread,
Yearning hearts take flight,
With dreams that will not shed.

A gentle touch ignites the flame,
With every whispered sigh,
Two souls entwined, none the same,
In a dance that feels so high.

Fingers trace along the skin,
A spark that lights the dark,
Embers fade, but love begins,
As passion leaves its mark.

In the silence, words unspoken,
Desires breathe through night,
Hearts' rhythm almost broken,
In love's most tender light.

A fleeting glance, a promise made,
In whispers soft and low,
Two spirits lost, yet unafraid,
In the warmth of love's glow.

Beneath the Shimmering Expanse

Stars are dancing in the sky,
Waves caress the shore,
Underneath, the night birds fly,
In a world we can't ignore.

The moonlight casts a silver hue,
On dreams that come alive,
In the shadow of night's blue,
We find where hearts can thrive.

Gentle breezes whisper sweet,
Carrying hopes afar,
With every pulse, our hearts repeat,
Beneath the same bright star.

In the hushed embrace of time,
We slip into the deep,
Each heartbeat, a sacred rhyme,
In the night, we dare to leap.

Beyond the veil of dusk and dawn,
We chase the dream we weave,
In twilight's glow, forever drawn,
By the beauty we believe.

The Dance of Blazing Hearts

Firelight flickers in the dark,
As shadows twist and twine,
Each moment holds a blazing spark,
Where passion starts to shine.

Bodies move in perfect flow,
In rhythm, fierce and wild,
With every glance, a fiery glow,
Love's dance is unreviled.

Laughter echoes through the night,
As hearts begin to race,
Two souls collide, a pure delight,
In love's intoxicating chase.

Every heartbeat sings a tune,
As sparks fly through the air,
Underneath the watchful moon,
We lose ourselves in flair.

Through every twirl, we find our way,
In the heat that we ignite,
In the dance where lovers play,
Hearts ablaze, spirits light.

Shadows of Sweet Temptation

In the twilight's gentle sigh,
Shadows whisper soft and low,
Desires lurking, oh so sly,
In the dance of ebb and flow.

Every glance from you I feel,
A pull that I can't fight,
In the dark, our hearts conceal,
Sweet temptations through the night.

Lips that promise hidden dreams,
Breath against my skin,
In the shadows, nothing seems,
To hold the thrill within.

Caught between the light and dark,
A choice we dare to make,
In this realm, we leave a mark,
As passions start to wake.

In the quiet, a spark ignites,
With every whispered name,
Through the shadows, pure delight,
In the dance that we claim.

Echoes of Forbidden Longing

In shadows deep, our secrets lie,
A yearning heart, a silent sigh.
Dreams woven tight, in night's embrace,
Two souls collide, yet time won't race.

A whispered touch, a glance unclaimed,
In secret nights, we stay unnamed.
Each heartbeat calls, in quiet despair,
A story written, no one can bear.

Against the tide, our fate we fight,
In creased silence, we seek the light.
Beneath the stars, our passion glows,
Yet in the dawn, we bear our woes.

The world outside refuses to see,
The bond we share, just you and me.
In stolen moments, love takes flight,
Echoes of longing, lost to the night.

In dreams we meet, where fears are gone,
A place to dance at dusk and dawn.
But with the day, the shadows come,
In echoes sweet, our love goes numb.

The Hidden Lantern of Love

Beneath the moon, a lantern glows,
Its gentle light, where no one knows.
In secret glades, our hearts entwined,
A hidden path, for souls aligned.

With every flicker, hope is found,
In whispered dreams that spin around.
We gather stardust, soft and bright,
To light the corners of the night.

Together we chase the fading dusk,
In gardens wild, where roses musk.
Every petal carries our tale,
Of love that blooms, and will prevail.

The dawn may come, but we'll remain,
With secrets held, through joy and pain.
The lantern's light will guide our way,
In hidden spaces, where hearts can sway.

So let the world keep turning still,
In soft embrace, we find our thrill.
For in the dark, we're never lost,
Our love's a lantern, never tossed.

Unspoken Songs of Affection

In silence, we sing with weary hearts,
A melody sweet, where love imparts.
No words are needed, just a glance,
In every beat, we find the dance.

The rhythm flows in quiet air,
A secret tune, beyond compare.
We weave our dreams, with threads of gold,
In uncharted paths, our souls unfold.

Through whispered nights, the stars align,
Our spirits soar, as we entwine.
An unspoken song, that knows no end,
In quiet moments, we transcend.

With every heartache, still we grow,
In every shadow, love will glow.
Though words remain, like drops of dew,
In silent songs, I cherish you.

So let our hearts compose the way,
In harmony, we'll find our play.
For unspoken songs will always guide,
The love we share, forever tied.

Caress of Breaking Dawn

As night surrenders to the day,
Soft whispers of light find their way.
The world awakens, a gentle play,
In tender hues, we start to sway.

The morning breeze, it breathes anew,
A canvas painted in vibrant hue.
With every ray, your touch I feel,
A promise bright, a love so real.

In caresses warm, the sun does rise,
Reflecting dreams in your eyes.
Each moment blooms, like flowers in spring,
With every dawn, our hearts take wing.

Through golden light, our spirits dance,
In every glance, a sweet romance.
From shadows deep, the light will draw,
In the caress of the dawn, we thaw.

So let the first light guide our way,
In tender warmth of new day's ray.
With every dawn, love's song is sung,
In the caress of morning, we are one.

The Language of Longing

In silence, hearts begin to speak,
Words unspoken, soft and meek.
Hope whispers through the midnight air,
A longing glance, a tender stare.

Time stretches thin, a fragile thread,
Promises dance in dreams unsaid.
Echoes of laughter in the night,
Each memory a flickering light.

Beneath the stars, desires bloom,
Filling shadows, chasing gloom.
Every heartbeat like a song,
In this language, we belong.

Fingers brush like softened rain,
In the quiet, we feel the pain.
Yet in the depths, hope glimmers bright,
Craving closeness, filling the night.

So let our souls find their way home,
In whispered verses, we will roam.
For every heartbeat speaks a name,
In longing's book, eternal flame.

Starlit Paths of Affection

Beneath vast skies, we walk alone,
Tracing starlit paths, unshown.
Each step a promise, bold and true,
Guided by love, our hearts renew.

The night wraps softly, like a shawl,
In the darkness, we hear the call.
With every twinkle, dreams ignite,
Lighting the way through endless night.

Gentle laughter fills the air,
A dance of shadows, free of care.
In this moment, time stands still,
Together we chase every thrill.

With fingers intertwined so tight,
We walk the starlit paths of light.
Each star a wish, a secret shared,
In love's embrace, we are prepared.

So let the universe conspire,
To feed our souls, to spark desire.
On starlit paths where hearts connect,
In affection's glow, we reflect.

Fires Beneath the Skin

A spark ignites, a flicker glows,
Deep within where passion grows.
Fires dance on skin so bare,
Whispers linger in the air.

Every glance fuels the flame,
A burning urge, no two the same.
Through shadows cast, our spirits fly,
In the heat where dreams defy.

The night ignites with every sigh,
As embers rise, we touch the sky.
With every heartbeat, flames ignite,
Together we embrace the night.

Beyond the world we once have known,
In passion's blaze, we've fully grown.
In the silence, our hearts will sing,
Of fires that warmth and fervor bring.

So let the world fade far away,
With every kiss, in dark we sway.
For in this heat, we find our way,
Fires beneath the skin will stay.

The Allure of Midnight Secrets

At midnight's hour, secrets creep,
Whispers linger, soft and deep.
In shadows cast, our truths unfold,
Mysteries wrapped in stories told.

Each glance a promise, laced in trust,
In the quiet, find the lust.
With every breath, the night reveals,
The hidden warmth that longing steals.

Underneath the silvered moon,
Hearts beat loudly, like a tune.
With every touch, we break the mold,
In this dance, our souls behold.

Entwined in dreams, where time stands still,
The thrill of secrets gives a thrill.
In every sigh, unspoken words,
Like fleeting dreams, like soaring birds.

But hold these truths, let them ignite,
In the depths of passion's light.
For midnight's allure, soft and sweet,
Keeps us tethered, hearts in retreat.

Echoing Hearts in the Twilight

In twilight's embrace, whispers weave,
Dreams dance softly, as shadows cleave.
Every heartbeat, a story untold,
In the fading light, our secrets unfold.

Stars awaken, one by one,
As night wraps around, the day is done.
With every echo, our spirits soar,
In the twilight glow, we crave for more.

Moonlight bathes us in silver hue,
Filling the air with memories anew.
Together we wander, lost in the night,
Echoing hearts in love's pure light.

The breeze carries tales, sweet and rare,
In the silence, soft sighs fill the air.
With each moment, we linger and sigh,
In twilight's embrace, where dreams never die.

Fingers entwined, we stand side by side,
In the hush of the night, our passions glide.
The world fades away, just you and I,
Echoing hearts beneath the vast sky.

Serenade of Unyielding Passion

In the hush of the night, a tune starts to play,
A serenade flows, guiding souls on their way.
Notes flutter softly like butterflies' wings,
In the heart of the night, where desire sings.

Lips brush gently, igniting the flame,
In a world of our own, unbound by the name.
Time stands still as our spirits entwine,
In this dance of passion, your heart beats with mine.

Stars burgeon above, witnesses bright,
To the symphony born in the stillness of night.
In the rhythm of love, we lose our refrain,
In pulses of ardor, we break every chain.

With every crescendo, emotions arise,
Reflections of longing surge in our eyes.
In the sweetness of moments, we forge our fate,
In the serenade's hold, we linger, not late.

Though the world may challenge what we hold dear,
In this flame of passion, we'll always draw near.
So let the music play on, bold and true,
In a serenade of love, just me and you.

The Taste of Forbidden Fruit

In shadows deep, a secret blooms,
Temptation lingers in hidden rooms.
With whispers shared in the hush of night,
The taste of forbidden, so sweet, so right.

Fingers brush softly, hearts race like the wind,
In this garden of longing, where fantasies begin.
Every glance exchanged ignites the spark,
In the depths of the dark, we both leave our mark.

Cloaked in silence, we steal every glance,
In this gamble of fate, we dare not take chance.
The allure of the unknown pulls us near,
The taste of forbidden, oh, so sincere.

Moments suspended, the clock ticks away,
Each breath shared, a bold display.
With every heartbeat, we dance on the edge,
In a world of desire, we make our pledge.

Though reason may beckon, we choose to defy,
For the taste of forbidden makes us feel high.
In the warmth of the night, our passion ignites,
In the sweetness of sin, love's true delight.

Cloak of Midnight Longing

Wrapped in the shadows, the night drapes around,
In the cloak of midnight, lost souls are found.
Each sigh carries dreams into the deep,
In the stillness of darkness, our secrets we keep.

With eyes like fire, we dance in the dark,
Every glance stolen, igniting a spark.
Midnight's embrace, a haunting caress,
In the cloak of longing, we find our rest.

Time flows like water, elusive and free,
In the depth of the night, just you and me.
A whisper, a promise, echoing low,
Underneath the cloak, our passions grow.

Lost in the magic that twilight bestows,
In the chill of the night, our desire flows.
Bound by the stars, we weave and we spin,
In the cloak of midnight, where dreams begin.

Through every heartbeat, the longing persists,
In the hush of the night, our hearts can't resist.
With each breath we take, enchantment is spun,
In the cloak of midnight, we are forever one.

Echoes of Transcendence

Whispers linger through the night,
Carried softly in the light.
Moments fleeting, lost in time,
Hearts entwined in silent rhyme.

Stars above begin to glow,
Guiding souls with gentle flow.
Threads of fate woven so tight,
Resonating with pure delight.

In the silence, truth unfurls,
A tapestry of hidden worlds.
Every echo tells a tale,
In the night where dreams prevail.

Mountains bow and rivers bend,
In the stillness, hearts ascend.
Through the chaos, we will find,
The peace that lies within the mind.

As we chase the fleeting dawn,
Fearing not what lies beyond.
Embrace the echoes, take your flight,
Transcend the shadows, reach the light.

Radiance in the Heart

In the stillness, love does bloom,
Casting shadows, dispelling gloom.
A flicker bright, so warm and clear,
It speaks to all who dare come near.

Gentle whispers in the air,
Breath of hope, a sacred prayer.
Eyes that glance, souls intertwine,
In this moment, all is divine.

Hold this light within your core,
Let it lead you to the shore.
Where the ocean meets the sky,
And dreams take wing, ready to fly.

Every heartbeat sings a song,
In its rhythm, we belong.
A melody of pure delight,
Guiding us through day and night.

Trust the radiance you feel,
In its glow, the world will heal.
As we dance beneath the stars,
Love will always conquer scars.

Luminous Dreams Unraveled

In the twilight, visions gleam,
Woven deeply into dreams.
Colors swirl, a vibrant view,
Opening paths to journeys new.

Every whisper, a spark ignites,
Chasing shadows, reaching heights.
Where the unknown starts to show,
A canvas born from heart's own flow.

Luminous thoughts begin to rise,
Revealing truths beneath the skies.
Casting light on what we seek,
Embracing all, both strong and weak.

With each heartbeat, dreams expand,
Guiding us with tender hand.
Every moment, rich and bright,
Unraveling the endless night.

Take a step into the glow,
Follow where the visions flow.
In this dance of light and shade,
Discover dreams that will not fade.

Embracing the Abyss

In the depths where shadows dwell,
Echoes of a silent spell.
Whispers haunting, voices low,
Yet within, a seed we sow.

Darkness calls, a siren's song,
As we wade where fears belong.
Yet in the depths there shines a grace,
Illuminating every space.

Hearts entwined in the unknown,
Finding strength we've never shown.
As we plunge into the dark,
A flicker bright ignites the spark.

With every breath, we take a stand,
Drawing courage from the land.
In the abyss, we find our way,
Transforming night into the day.

Embrace the void, for it will teach,
Lessons only dreams can reach.
In the darkness, truth will rise,
A radiant dawn in painted skies.

Ephemeral Flames of Want

Flickers dance in shadows dark,
Desires whisper, leaving a mark.
Hearts ignite in fleeting glow,
Yearning for what we cannot know.

Moments sigh, like smoke they fade,
In silence, dreams of love parade.
Eager hands, yet tempests churn,
What we crave, for it we yearn.

Fleeting touches, breathless grace,
In a heartbeat, we find our place.
The fire burns but does it last?
In the night, ambitions cast.

Hope ignites a softer plea,
Lost in the flames of what could be.
A fleeting glance, the spark ignites,
As passion fades with fading lights.

From ashes rise the echoes sweet,
Yet all we have is bittersweet.
In the end, what's left to claim,
But whispers of an unseen flame.

Beyond the Silken Curtains

Behind the drapes, a world unseen,
Whispers linger, where we have been.
Shadows dance in borrowed light,
Secrets held in velvet night.

A rustle soft, the fabric sways,
Echoes of forgotten days.
Promises made, but never told,
In the silence, stories unfold.

In every fold, a dream resides,
Wishing for what the heart confides.
The outside world may seem so bright,
Yet here, our dreams take flight.

Exploring realms beyond the seams,
Lost in the weave of tender dreams.
I offer you a glimpse of grace,
A hidden truth in this secret space.

Beneath the sheen, love softly glows,
In whispered breaths, our longing grows.
With every thread, a promise waits,
To reveal what fate creates.

Threads of Electric Connection

Wires hum with a silent song,
In this space, we both belong.
Electric sparks in every glance,
Weaving fate in fleeting chance.

Kilohertz of the heart's delight,
Euphoria ignites the night.
Through signals lost and found again,
Connections made, the soul's refrain.

Dots and lines drawn through the air,
In this web, love's muse lays bare.
Infinite paths intertwine,
In every pulse, your heart is mine.

Power surges, bright and swift,
In this moment, bliss is the gift.
We build a world of unseen ties,
In echoes, our affection lies.

Together, we embrace the vibe,
Waves colliding, we come alive.
Through the chaos, we will find,
Electric dreams forever bind.

Yearning in the Moonlight

Beneath the glow, our secrets stir,
In silvery beams, hearts start to blur.
Moonlit paths where shadows drift,
In this dance, our spirits lift.

Soft whispers on a gentle breeze,
A moment's peace, desire's tease.
Lost in dreams where lovers vow,
With silent hearts, we breathe the now.

The night wraps us in tender grace,
As stars bear witness to our embrace.
Each heartbeat echoes through the dark,
In your eyes, I find my spark.

The world stands still while time unwinds,
As longing binds where love reminds.
Underneath this vast expanse,
In moonlight soft, we find our chance.

Yearning paints the canvas wide,
With every breath, the truth won't hide.
In the moon's embrace, we ignite,
Two souls woven, lost in night.

The Rhythm of Abandoned Desires

In shadows where whispers abide,
Dreams linger, nowhere to hide.
Faded echoes dance in the night,
Hushed memories fade from sight.

Heartbeats thrummed in silent despair,
Chasing ghosts that linger in air.
Longing calls through the midnight stream,
A barren field where we once dreamed.

Yearning sparks like a fleeting flame,
Passions shift, yet it feels the same.
Choices made that led us astray,
Lost in the rhythm, we fade away.

Unwritten songs on parchment bare,
In every note, a longing stare.
Cadence sways like leaves in spring,
While time slips gently on velvet wing.

Faded glories, the heart still sings,
In the silence, the past still clings.
A melody of what was once true,
In the ruins of dreams, I search for you.

The Muse of Secret Pleasures

Beneath the moon's soft, watchful gaze,
Whispers linger in twilight haze.
Veils of mystery on lips so sweet,
In hidden corners, our shadows meet.

Laughter dances on breathless air,
Secrets shared without a care.
In the quiet, our hearts entwine,
Finding bliss in the soft divine.

Whirling thoughts like petals in flight,
Unfolding wonders of pure delight.
A canvas of dreams in tender hues,
Painting moments that love imbues.

Tangled sheets and whispered sighs,
In your eyes, the universe lies.
Wrapped in warmth, time stands still,
As desires rise to flood and fill.

Golden threads of passion weave,
In your embrace, I truly believe.
This secret world that we've spun tight,
A treasure found in the cloak of night.

Veins of Starlit Passion

In the dark of night, we ignite,
Veins of passion, a blazing light.
Stars collide in cosmic dance,
Each heartbeat pulls us into trance.

Brighter than dreams, our spirits soar,
Woven together, forevermore.
A tapestry of endless dreams,
In midnight's embrace, our love redeems.

Fires linger in the pale moon's glow,
In this realm, only we can know.
Whispers of fate entwined in fate,
A love so deep, it transcends fate.

Through galaxies, our souls entwined,
In every star, our hearts aligned.
Drawing from depths of the astral sea,
Passion flows through you and me.

In voids of silence, our echoes play,
A starlit path, we'll find our way.
The dance of ages unspoken here,
Will forever shine, drawing us near.

Rippled Waters of a Quiet Yearning

Beneath the surface, ripples spread,
A quiet yearning, softly bred.
Waves of longing in twilight's sheen,
Where dreams once swayed, now tranquil green.

Glimmers dance on a gentle tide,
Each reflection, a world to confide.
In whispered dreams, we drift anew,
In the silence, I'll wait for you.

Moonlit secrets kiss the shore,
With every tide, I want you more.
The still waters hold tales untold,
Of hearts so brave, yet feeling cold.

In the quiet, shadows play,
A longing pulse that will not sway.
Rippling echoes, a heart's soft plea,
In the depths of night, just you and me.

As dawn approaches, silvery light,
Awakens dreams that drifted in night.
Together we'll ride each wave and turn,
In these waters, forever yearn.

Flickering Tides of Emotion

Waves crash softly on the shore,
A dance of feelings, evermore.
Beneath the surface, shadows hide,
The heart's deep currents, a ceaseless tide.

Moments shimmer in twilight's glow,
Each flicker tells tales we know.
The pull and push of love and fear,
In tides of sorrow, joy draws near.

Seagulls call, a haunting sound,
As whispers mate with ocean's bound.
Emotions swell like storms at sea,
Fleeting and fierce, they set us free.

Caught in a cycle, endlessly spun,
The ebbing daylight, day is done.
We ride the waves, a fragile thread,
In depths where all our hopes are fed.

Yet still we linger, watch the hue,
Of water painted in gold and blue.
For in these flickering tides we find,
The essence of our heart and mind.

Coals of Incessant Dreams

In the quiet of the night,
Flickering spirits take their flight.
Whispers rise from embers' glow,
As wishes dance, and hopes bestow.

A spark ignites a brilliant flame,
Illuminating hearts with name.
Dreams tread softly, wear no chains,
Through darkened paths, love's light remains.

Shadows linger where we tread,
In corridors of thoughts unsaid.
Yet still we chase the fleeting blaze,
In coals of dreams, we weave our maze.

With every breath, we keep them close,
These fiery visions, passions gross.
Though flames may flicker, hearts ignite,
A warmth emerges from the night.

So let us stoke this burning fire,
And let our souls reach ever higher.
For in the warmth of dreams aglow,
We find the strength to heal and grow.

Ribbons of Ecstasy Unfurled

Colors dance in morning light,
Ribbons flutter, a joyful sight.
They swirl and spin, a vibrant trace,
In each embrace, we find our space.

Notes of laughter fill the air,
With every heartbeat, without care.
Unfurled delights that thrill the soul,
In moments fleeting, we are whole.

Whispers weave through summer's breeze,
Entwined in joy, hearts find their ease.
Each thread of bliss a story told,
In shimmering hues, we break the mold.

A tapestry of dreams we share,
With every gaze, we catch the flare.
United in the dance of fate,
We paint our world, we celebrate.

So let the ribbons sway and rise,
Embracing life in all its guise.
With ecstasy our guiding star,
Together, love, we'll wander far.

A Journey of Sultry Whispers

A breeze caresses, soft and warm,
In twilight's glow, our souls transform.
Through sultry nights, silence speaks,
With whispers shared, the heartache leaks.

Underneath the moon's soft gaze,
We weave our thoughts in smoky haze.
Secrets linger on tender lips,
In every sigh, the heart eclipses.

As shadows dance, we hold on tight,
Lost in the magic of the night.
A journey woven with every breath,
In the hush, we find our depth.

Tender moments, fleeting, rare,
As starlit dreams float in the air.
In whispers close, our spirits meld,
Through sultry warmth, our love is held.

So take my hand, let's drift away,
Into the night where we will stay.
In whispered tales and softest sighs,
Together, love, we'll touch the skies.

The Allure Beneath the Surface

Beneath the calm, a current flows,
Soft whispers weave where shadows doze.
Secrets hide in depths unseen,
Mysteries swirl in shades of green.

With gentle tides, the heart explores,
Each ripple tells of distant shores.
The treasure lies in silent grace,
A world unfolds in hidden space.

Moonlight dances on the waves,
Guiding dreams in watery caves.
Thoughts drift like leaves on summer air,
Embracing peace, without a care.

Echoes linger, tales unfold,
A tapestry of stories told.
The allure is deep, enchanting, bright,
A siren's call in the soft twilight.

In the stillness, truth reveals,
A spirit captured, time conceals.
The dance of life beneath the tide,
Where all the wonders like to hide.

The Scent of Hidden Fires

In the woods, the embers glow,
Whispers of heat in the breeze that blow.
Each flicker breathes life anew,
As shadows play in dusky hue.

Sparks arise from threads undone,
Filling the air with tales of fun.
On nights where stillness claims the sky,
The scent of warmth makes spirits fly.

Through the branches, light breaks free,
Carrying dreams on paths of glee.
An unseen magic guides the night,
While hearts are drawn to the flickering light.

Hidden stories in the blaze,
Moments linger, time decays.
With every spark, a wish takes flight,
Dancing gently, pure delight.

As the day surrenders, fades,
Fires burn strong, weaving cascades.
In the darkness, hope inspires,
Awakening the scent of hidden fires.

Dreamcatcher of Infinite Possibilities

Woven threads in twilight's weave,
Capture dreams that night conceive.
A realm where wishes softly spin,
Boundless worlds where hopes begin.

In starry paths, the visions flow,
Drawing light where futures glow.
Each whispered thought, a gentle breeze,
Weaving magic 'neath ancient trees.

Feathers drift on cosmic winds,
Guiding souls where adventure begins.
A tapestry of thoughts and schemes,
Conceiving life from vibrant dreams.

As dawn awakens the silent night,
The dreamer's heart takes flight in light.
Each possibility, a chance to find,
The dreams that weave within the mind.

So cast your hopes upon the sky,
Let your spirit soar and fly.
For in the vastness, realize,
Your dreams will bloom and rise.

The Secret Breath of Moonlit Nights

In the hush of night, the world holds sway,
Moonlight whispers, softly blurs the day.
A cool embrace in shadowed glades,
Where dreams entwine in silken shades.

The stars align in subtle grace,
Each glimmer paints a cosmic space.
Breath of secrets, softly laid,
In the dark, our fears will fade.

Gentle winds play through the leaves,
Carrying stories time retrieves.
With every sigh, a new tale penned,
The night unfolds, a timeless friend.

Awake the heart to magic's flow,
As quiet thoughts begin to grow.
Embrace the peace the darkness weaves,
Within the night, a spirit believes.

For in the moon's soft, silver light,
The world transforms into pure sight.
Breathe deep the mystic, sweet delight,
In the secret breath of moonlit night.

Veins of Temptation

In shadows deep, whispers call,
Where dreams and desires intertwine.
Flesh and spirit, they rise and fall,
In the dance of the divine.

Promises linger, sweetened sighs,
As hearts beat in a timeless race.
With every breath, the passion flies,
Capturing us in its embrace.

Echoes of lust in the moonlit air,
Pulse quickening, we lose control.
We revel in this potent dare,
Bound tight between body and soul.

Moments wrapped in silken threads,
Seduction's grip, a potent spell.
Tracing paths where longing treads,
In the haven where lovers dwell.

Veins of temptation constrict and pull,
A fervent surge, no retreat.
Awash in desire, hearts are full,
Until the dawn, we feel complete.

Chasing the Infinite

Stars align in the vast expanse,
A canvas where dreams are drawn.
With every hope, we take our chance,
To dance with the endless dawn.

Waves of wonder crash and swell,
Upon shores of the unknown.
Whispers of fate, they softly tell,
Of paths we've never flown.

We chase the light through fleeting time,
Tracing echoes of our past.
With hearts aflame, we dare to climb,
To horizons that hold us fast.

Journeying deep into the void,
Where silence sings its haunting tune.
Through every fear, the heart's employed,
A spirit danced beneath the moon.

Each moment, a thread in the weave,
Of a tapestry, ever bold.
In the chase, it's love we believe,
As stories of old are retold.

Tides of Sensual Reverie

In twilight's grasp, we are reborn,
Where whispers linger in the air.
With every touch, sweet heat is sworn,
As bodies sway in quiet prayer.

Sea salt and skin, a mingled fate,
Waves break softly on sands of time.
With every pulse, we create,
A rhythm, a sultry rhyme.

Desire blooms like a night-blooming flower,
In twilight's dream, we lose our way.
With every breath, we feel the power,
As night turns gently into day.

In a dance of shadows, we find our truth,
Lost in the depths of uncharted bliss.
The taste of longing, a timeless youth,
In the maw of a passionate kiss.

Rising and falling, waves of delight,
With every touch, we dive and soar.
In tides so deep, we take flight,
Forever caught in love's encore.

The Canvas of Connection

Two hearts brush against the night,
In colors clashing, soft and bright.
Each glance a stroke, each laugh a shade,
On this canvas, love is made.

From whispered dreams, our portraits grow,
In harmony, our spirits flow.
With every meeting, depth expands,
In this masterpiece, we hold hands.

Textures mingle, bold and soft,
A tapestry hung in the loft.
Moments captured, etched in time,
In vibrant hues, our hearts entwine.

Through storms and sun, we paint anew,
With every challenge, our love drew.
In every stroke, the truth unspoken,
Connections forged, never broken.

With every hue, our story shines,
On this canvas, love defines.
United, we create our fate,
In art, in heart, we celebrate.

The Language of Delicate Touches

Fingers trace the silent air,
A gentle brush, a fleeting care.
Hearts collide in soft embrace,
In every touch, a secret space.

Whispers linger on the skin,
Every gesture, where love begins.
Echoes dance in twilight's glow,
In quiet realms, feelings flow.

Laughter melts in tender light,
As shadows pulse with pure delight.
Moments captured, delicate, sweet,
In this language, souls compete.

Eyes that speak, when words fall shy,
In hidden depths, we learn to fly.
Each caress, a silent vow,
In tender frames, we live the now.

Softest sighs in twilight's weave,
In every touch, our hearts believe.
With gentle warmth, we start anew,
In delicate dreams, I find you.

Veins of Heat in a Chilled Night

In the dark, our breaths unite,
Veins pulse warm, igniting light.
Chilled winds wrap the world outside,
But in this space, love cannot hide.

Stars shiver in the frosted air,
Yet here, we gather without care.
Skin on skin in whispered hush,
In every heartbeat, a soft rush.

Veins of heat coursing through,
With every gaze, the night feels new.
Outside, shadows play and mock,
Inside, we build a solid block.

Fires warm our hidden dreams,
In silent glances, love redeems.
Echoes dance beneath the moon,
In this rapture, hearts attune.

Rest your head and drift away,
Let dreams ignite the break of day.
In pure connection, we find peace,
In chilled nights, our fires increase.

Resonance of Dreamlike Whispers

Beneath the stars, the secrets flow,
In echoes soft, they come and go.
Dreamlike whispers, sweet and low,
In quiet corners, feelings grow.

Through haze of dusk, the shadows sway,
In silent murmurs, we find our way.
Every word, a gentle sigh,
A promise held, a soft goodbye.

In twilight's veil, our stories blend,
Resonating, they transcend.
In every laugh, in every tear,
Whispers linger, ever near.

Hearts entwined in soft embrace,
We dance in dreams, a sacred space.
Resonance of all we share,
In whispers light as thin air.

When morning breaks, and shadows flee,
In every glance, you're still with me.
Through dreamlike waves, love flows and swells,
In whisper's magic, our story dwells.

The Labyrinth of Heartbeats

In winding paths where echoes blend,
The labyrinth beckons, twists, extends.
Every heartbeat marks the way,
In this maze where we will stay.

Rhythms pulse within our frame,
Wandering souls, igniting flame.
With every turn, I hear your name,
In this dance, we play our game.

Labyrinths of love and fear,
In shadows deep, you feel me near.
Chasing dreams through narrow halls,
In your whispers, my heart calls.

Every chamber holds a truth,
In every breath, we share our youth.
Winding corners, bright and dark,
In this maze, we find our spark.

Through tangled paths, we make our course,
A timeless bond, our strongest force.
In the labyrinth, we are free,
With heartbeats speaking endlessly.

The Pulse of Enchanted Nights

In twilight's embrace, whispers entwine,
Stars flicker softly, a dance so divine.
Moonlight reflects on dreams yet to be,
Casting a glow on hearts wild and free.

Gentle winds carry tales from afar,
Every heartbeat echoes, a fleeting star.
Under the canopy of velvet skies,
Magic ignites as the night softly sighs.

Shadows twirl in a waltz of delight,
As fireflies shimmer, igniting the night.
Breathless moments linger, pure and bright,
Weaving together our souls in the light.

The pulse of the night, a rhythm so true,
Guides us through paths where wishes accrue.
In the heart of the night, we chase the call,
Embracing the whispers, we rise and we fall.

Together we wander, lost in the dream,
In the pulse of enchanted, we become a theme.
The night wraps us in its silken embrace,
In a realm where time leaves not a trace.

Ruins of Long-Lost Emotions

Amidst crumbled walls, echoes still sigh,
In the heart of the ruins where memories lie.
Time painted sorrow, yet beauty remains,
In the heart of the shadows, love's tender chains.

Each stone tells a story, of laughter and tears,
Beneath all the moss, there lingered the years.
The whispers of passion, now echoes of pain,
In the ruins of love, memories sustain.

Sunlight breaks gently, revealing the past,
Faded photographs, a moment not lost.
Roots intertwine where the heartstrings were played,
Long-lost emotions in silence displayed.

Though walls have collapsed, hope still finds a way,
Resilience gathers, forging light from decay.
From the ashes of sorrow rises the dawn,
In the ruins of feelings, new dreams are drawn.

So wander these remnants, embrace every trace,
For love's tender ruins still hold a sweet grace.
In the shadows of heartache, the future ignites,
In the ruins of emotions, new love reunites.

Threads of Enchantment's Fabric

In the loom of existence, threads intertwine,
Colors of magic, a tapestry divine.
Whispers of secrets in patterns so bright,
Stitching together the day and the night.

Each thread spun with dreams of those yet to come,
Binding together the hum of the drum.
In every knot lies a promise, a wish,
Echoes of longing, a warm, tender kiss.

From bright golden mornings to silvery moons,
The fabric of time hums forgotten tunes.
Woven in layers, our stories combine,
Life's vibrant spectrum, a tapestry fine.

Frayed edges whisper of journeys begun,
In the threads of enchantment, our hearts become one.
Dances of fate in a vibrant parade,
Every stitch telling tales of love never frayed.

So hold tight the fabric that binds us each day,
In the threads of enchantment, forever we'll stay.
For woven together, through laughter and strife,
The fabric of dreams is the essence of life.

Whirlwind of Hidden Fantasies

In a storm of emotion, fantasies swirl,
Dreams take flight in a shimmering whirl.
Caught in the breeze of what might yet be,
Hidden desires sing sweet lullabies free.

Each thought like a leaf, tossed up to the sky,
Twirling on currents where butterflies fly.
In the chaos of longing, visions appear,
A whirlwind of wishes igniting the sphere.

Voices of passion echo through the night,
As shadows dance lightly, hearts take to flight.
Whispers of courage entangled in time,
Navigating secrets, life's beautiful rhyme.

With every rotation, new paths we embrace,
In a whirlwind of dreams, we find our place.
Hidden ambitions come alive in the storm,
A tapestry woven where hearts can transform.

So release your spirit, let it take wing,
In the whirlwind of fantasies, let your soul sing.
For within every gust, there's a chance to ignite,
The magic of dreams that await in the night.

Secrets in the Ember Glow

Whispers dance in twilight's fire,
Fragmented dreams rise higher.
In the shadows, secrets sing,
Underneath the night's soft wing.

Embers flicker, stories unfold,
Tales of warmth, of hearts bold.
Beneath the sky's deepening hue,
A world of wonder, pure and true.

Glimmers of hope, they intertwine,
In the silence, a spark divine.
Each flicker tells of love's embrace,
A journey through time, a gentle place.

In the night, the stars align,
Holding secrets, dark and fine.
The ember glow, a guiding light,
Leading souls through the night.

So hold these secrets, let them flow,
In the warmth of the ember glow.
For therein lies a truth untold,
A flame within, a heart of gold.

Veils of Enchantment

In the garden where shadows play,
Whispers weave throughout the day.
Veils of enchantment softly fall,
A mystical touch, a beckoning call.

Petals dance in the gentle breeze,
Carrying secrets among the trees.
Every rustling leaf holds a dream,
A moonlit spell, a silver beam.

Time stands still, in golden hour,
Each moment blooming like a flower.
Veils of enchantment, tenderly spun,
In this sanctuary, we become one.

Let the magic wrap around,
In this space, our souls are found.
With every glance, a spark ignites,
In the heart of these enchanted nights.

So linger here, where dreams align,
In the veils of enchantment, you'll find.
A tapestry of love and grace,
In this enchanted, timeless place.

The Radiance of Entwined Souls

Two hearts beat in harmony's song,
A thread of light that pulls them strong.
In radiant colors, they embrace,
Dance of love, a fervent grace.

Stars align, their paths converge,
In every glance, a gentle surge.
Entwined souls wrapped in affection,
A symphony of pure connection.

Whispers in the quiet night,
Together they shine, a wondrous sight.
In every heartbeat, a tale unfolds,
A story of love, forever bold.

Through valleys deep, o'er mountains high,
With every breath, they soar and fly.
The radiance warms, an endless glow,
In the bond where true love flows.

So cherish the spark, let it ignite,
In the radiance of endless light.
For in their hearts, a blaze remains,
The dance of love, through joy and pains.

Breath of a Silent Serenade

In the hush of twilight's breath,
A serenade of life and death.
Soft murmurs weave through the trees,
Carried gently on the breeze.

Notes unspoken fill the air,
A lullaby kissed by despair.
In the silence, echoes abound,
The heart's rhythm, a tender sound.

Every whisper, a tale unsung,
In the twilight, where dreams are flung.
Moments linger, time suspended,
In the quiet, hearts are blended.

So close your eyes, let go of strife,
Feel the pulse of vibrant life.
In the stillness, find your way,
In the breath of this silent play.

Embrace the night, let shadows roam,
For in this serenade, you're home.
With every heartbeat, every sigh,
A melody that will never die.

The Secrets of Tangled Souls

In shadows deep, we intertwine,
Whispers soft, a sacred sign.
The threads of fate, they twist and bend,
A silent pact, where lovers mend.

Beneath the stars, our secrets lie,
With every glance, a silent sigh.
In tangled dreams, we find our way,
A dance of souls, in night and day.

The world may fade, but we remain,
Two hearts entwined in joy and pain.
In every heartbeat, echoes speak,
The strength we find when we are weak.

Through storms we walk, hand in hand,
A journey carved in shifting sand.
We'll brave the dark, for love's embrace,
And find our home in one sweet place.

As years go by, our whispers grow,
A melody only we can know.
The secrets shared, forever whole,
The timeless bond of tangled souls.

Ripples of a Daring Promise

In the moonlight's gentle glow,
A promise made, we let it flow.
With every breath, our hopes take flight,
Ripples dance in the quiet night.

The courage found in whispered dreams,
Unfolding truth, or so it seems.
With hearts ablaze, we dare to stand,
Embracing fate, hand in hand.

In every tear, a story told,
Of battles fought, and hopes turned gold.
We'll forge ahead, where others flee,
For in this dance, we are set free.

Through winds of change, our spirits soar,
With every step, we seek for more.
In silence shared, a promise grows,
Ripples formed by the love we chose.

The tides may rise, yet still we trust,
In every challenge, love is a must.
Together we'll find the strength we need,
Ripples echoing every deed.

Hues of Desire Under Starlight

The night unfolds in colors bright,
Whispers soft, beneath starlight.
In every glance, a fire ignites,
Hues of desire, daring flights.

The world asleep, but passion wakes,
With tender hearts, the silence breaks.
We paint the sky with dreams so bold,
In shades of love, our stories told.

Each star a promise, shining clear,
A symphony that draws us near.
With every touch, the canvas blooms,
A masterpiece in darkly rooms.

The moonlight wraps us in its grace,
A fleeting moment, time can't chase.
In hues of fire, our spirits blend,
Under starlight, we shall transcend.

As dusk turns dawn, our colors fade,
Yet in our hearts, the essence stayed.
Through whispered dreams, and silent sighs,
In hues of desire, love never dies.

Unveiling the Depths of Longing

In quiet corners, shadows play,
Yearning hearts find their way.
Echoes linger, soft and low,
Unveiling depths we rarely show.

With every heartbeat, secrets rise,
The flames of passion in our sighs.
In whispered dreams, we seek to find,
The threads that bind two souls aligned.

Through veils of doubt, our spirits dance,
In fleeting moments, we take the chance.
With every kiss, the layers peel,
Unraveling truths we dare to feel.

The tides of time may try to sway,
Yet in your gaze, I long to stay.
Together we chase the dreams of night,
Unveiling depths, in shared light.

In the silence where love abides,
All fears dissolve, our hearts confide.
For in this journey, hand in hand,
We unveil the depths where love stands.

Unveiling the Flame

In the quiet night, embers glow,
Whispers of dreams begin to flow.
A flicker ignites the heart's delight,
Unveiling the flame, chasing the night.

Dancing shadows, secrets shared,
With every touch, souls unpaired.
Heat of passion, a blazing spark,
Unveiling the flame, guiding in dark.

Softly spoken words of care,
Two hearts entwined, a perfect pair.
The light of love, forever bright,
Unveiling the flame, lit with insight.

Through trials faced, storms may rise,
Yet love will soar, reaching the skies.
Together, we'll keep the fire near,
Unveiling the flame, banishing fear.

Threads of Intimacy

In gentle moments, our fingers twine,
Together we weave a love divine.
Threads of intimacy, strong and bold,
Stories etched in warmth untold.

Eyes that linger, whispers shared,
Every glance, our hearts laid bare.
Stitching dreams with tenderness true,
Threads of intimacy, me and you.

Soft breaths mingle in the air,
Creating a bond that we both share.
Wrapped in each other's arms so tight,
Threads of intimacy, pure delight.

In the silence, connections grow,
A silent promise, a steady flow.
In each heartbeat, our love imbues,
Threads of intimacy, forever fused.

Beneath the Surface of Love

Beneath the surface, silence speaks,
In hidden depths, our longing peaks.
Silent currents, a gentle tide,
Beneath the surface, where hearts collide.

Hidden treasures lie below,
In the stillness, passions grow.
Unseen layers of dreams we chase,
Beneath the surface, a warm embrace.

With every look, stories unfold,
Whispers of secrets, tender and bold.
In quiet moments, we find our place,
Beneath the surface, love's soft grace.

Waves may crash, storms may wane,
Yet we dive deep through joy and pain.
In the depths, we'll find our way,
Beneath the surface, love will stay.

The Pulse of Hidden Yearnings

In the stillness, desires wake,
A heartbeat quickens, real or fake?
The pulse of hidden yearnings rise,
A dance of shadows in the skies.

Every glance, a tethered thread,
Words unspoken, a life unsaid.
Embers flicker, longing blooms,
The pulse of hidden yearnings looms.

In quiet moments, dreams ignite,
A flickering spark in the night.
Each sigh a promise yet uncried,
The pulse of hidden yearnings, untried.

Through the noise, our truth we hear,
In the chaos, we persevere.
Navigating feelings, raw and pure,
The pulse of hidden yearnings, secure.

Chasing Shadows of Forgotten Dreams

In the whisper of the night, we roam,
Searching for echoes of what felt like home.
Moonlight dances on paths long past,
Only shadows of dreams that couldn't last.

Each step a reminder, each sigh a call,
Of hopes that once soared but began to fall.
We chase the flickers that lead us back,
To memories buried under time's attack.

Yet in the silence, a spark still glows,
A thread of passion, the heart still knows.
Through the mist, we feel the gentle pull,
Of dreams entwined, forever beautiful.

Though some might fade as dawn approaches,
In the chase, we discover, life broaches.
Through shadows we tread, we learn to find,
The beauty in places that once seemed blind.

So let us wander, let hearts be free,
In chasing shadows, we find the key.
For every dream must rise and fall,
Yet in their remnants, we feel it all.

Flourish of Entangled Love

In tangled roots, our hearts did bind,
A love that grows, both sweet and blind.
Like vines that weave and dance in air,
Each moment shared, a thread to wear.

Sunlight spills on dreams we weave,
In the warmth of trust, we dare believe.
Together we blossom, through rain and shine,
A garden flourishing, yours and mine.

With every petal, a promise made,
In colors bright, our fears do fade.
Entwined in laughter, in joy we bask,
In the beauty of love, no need to ask.

Seasons change, yet we remain,
In the tender echoes of joy and pain.
A dance of hearts, a gentle sigh,
In this entangled love, we forever lie.

So hold my hand, let time stand still,
In nature's splendor, we find our thrill.
Together we flourish, a bond so grand,
Entangled in love, forever we stand.

The Allure of Fleeting Glances

In crowded rooms, our eyes collide,
A spark ignites, with nowhere to hide.
Fleeting glances, moments sustain,
In the silence, we share the same pain.

Each time our paths brush, a story unfolds,
In the depth of a look, a thousand tales told.
A lingering gaze suggests an embrace,
In the dance of the night, we find our place.

Yet shadows loom, as daylight breaks,
With every goodbye, a heart still aches.
In the allure of what could have been,
We chase the dream, the moment unseen.

Still, in the rush, a heartbeat remains,
In the chase for more, love entertains.
Fleeting but real, it leaves us enmeshed,
In glances exchanged, we find our quest.

So let us savor, these moments divine,
In the allure of glances, your heart next to mine.
For every brief encounter that passes by,
Is a glimpse of love that dares to fly.

Veiled Glimpses of Us

In the shadows, where whispers dwell,
Veiled glimpses of us, a silent spell.
Through curtain folds, our secrets stray,
Caught in the twilight, where dreams lay.

A quiet touch, the brush of knuckles,
In fleeting moments, the heart still chuckles.
Unseen smiles hidden in the night,
In veiled glances, everything feels right.

Each secret meeting, the world fades away,
In the dance of shadows, together we sway.
With every heartbeat, a tale we share,
In veiled glimpses, love is laid bare.

Yet time is cruel, it steals the light,
Leaving us yearning for what feels right.
But in these veils, we find our song,
In the melody of us, we can't be wrong.

So let us cherish each hidden tune,
In the veils of twilight, we find our moon.
For love's true essence, though often concealed,
In glimpses of us, our hearts are revealed.

The Canvas of Intimate Desires

Brushstrokes of longing dance on the page,
Colors entwined, a vibrant wage.
Whispers of dreams in delicate hue,
Crafting a world where love feels true.

Silk threads weave through shadows and light,
Every touch soft, a beautiful sight.
In the silence, secrets are spun,
A tapestry tells of two becoming one.

With every layer, depth grows strong,
In the stillness, our hearts belong.
Each curve and line a story told,
Passions ignite, as we dare to be bold.

As night descends, the canvas glows,
Embracing desires the heart knows.
In this gallery of dreams we reside,
Drawn together, we cannot hide.

With every stroke, a new chance waits,
The canvas calls, as fate creates.
Lost in hues of fervent embrace,
In artful love, we find our place.

Harvest Moon of Secret Yearnings

Under the moon, ripe fears abound,
Silent whispers rise from the ground.
Fields of wishes, aching and sweet,
Gathered beneath the night's heartbeat.

Each shadowed path we dare to roam,
Guided by dreams that lead us home.
Secrets hidden among the trees,
Swaying softly in the midnight breeze.

Crickets sing of love's embrace,
While fireflies twinkle, illuminating space.
Hands entwined, we share our fate,
Under the glow, we contemplate.

The air is thick with hope and sighs,
Yearning gazes and soft replies.
Together we dance, the stars align,
In the harvest's bounty, our spirits entwine.

As dawn approaches, shadows will fade,
But in our hearts, this night is made.
Forever we'll cherish the moon's soft light,
In secret yearnings that feel so right.

Pulse of the Hidden Heart

Beneath the surface, a rhythm beats,
Yearning echoes, soft in retreats.
In silence, the heart speaks loud and clear,
Carrying secrets we hold dear.

Fleeting moments in a crowded space,
Caught in the web of a knowing glance.
Every heartbeat a silent vow,
Creating a bond we can't allow.

Tides of emotion swell and flow,
Mapping the places where love will go.
In shadows we linger, heart to heart,
Finding solace as secrets start.

The pulse of love, a steady sound,
In hidden corners, together we're found.
With every whisper, our spirits soar,
A timeless dance on an endless floor.

In the quiet, our souls ignite,
A spark of hope in the darkest night.
Together we weave, a sacred art,
Eternal echoes of the hidden heart.

Nectar of the Unseen

In gardens rich, sweetness resides,
Petals open where passion hides.
A fragrant breeze whispers your name,
Drawing us close, staking our claim.

Cascades of laughter, rivers of light,
Flowing together, a delicious sight.
Each moment savored, a tender kiss,
In the nectar of love, we find our bliss.

From the depths of our souls, desire flows,
Filling the spaces where silence grows.
With every taste, we long for more,
In this sanctuary, we both explore.

Unseen connections binding us tight,
A dance of shadows in the moonlight.
Every heartbeat a promise made,
In your embrace, uncertainties fade.

As the sun sets, and darkness falls,
We gather the dreams that the night recalls.
In the nectar of unseen bliss,
Every encounter, a moment we miss.

www.ingramcontent.com/pod-product-compliance
Lightning Source LLC
Chambersburg PA
CBHW071611290125
21070CB00033B/1143